Angela Verges has the unique ability to analyze what is difficult and pull the threads of scripture and experience that lead to victory. This book is for all those sisters who recognize that the biological ups and downs of menopause can impact a woman's walk with Christ. Angela Verges brilliant sense of humor helps soothe the struggle.

– George Waddles Jr.- Pastor, Second Baptist Church, Ypsilanti, MI

Angie has a very creative sense of humor. Her performances have been riveting, and full of consistent wit. Her menopause performance is hilarious, and relatable. Her ability to write relative material for a large viewing audience is one of her strong attributes.

- Iris aka Ms. Gee, Comedian

MENOPAUSE
AIN'T NO JOKE

Blending Faith and Humor in
Perfectly Imperfect Situations

ANGELA VERGES

WESTBOW
PRESS®
A DIVISION OF THOMAS NELSON
& ZONDERVAN

This book is a work of non-fiction. Unless otherwise noted, the author and the publisher
make no explicit guarantees as to the accuracy of the information contained in this book
and in some cases, names of people and places have been altered to protect their privacy.

WestBow Press books may be ordered through booksellers or by contacting:

WestBow Press
A Division of Thomas Nelson & Zondervan
1663 Liberty Drive
Bloomington, IN 47403
www.westbowpress.com
1 (866) 928-1240

Because of the dynamic nature of the Internet, any web addresses or links contained in
this book may have changed since publication and may no longer be valid. The views
expressed in this work are solely those of the author and do not necessarily reflect the
views of the publisher, and the publisher hereby disclaims any responsibility for them.

Any people depicted in stock imagery provided by Getty Images are models,
and such images are being used for illustrative purposes only.
Certain stock imagery © Getty Images.

ISBN: 978-1-9736-4601-3 (sc)
ISBN: 978-1-9736-4602-0 (hc)
ISBN: 978-1-9736-4600-6 (e)

Library of Congress Control Number: 2018913813

Print information available on the last page.

WestBow Press rev. date: 12/03/2018

For Reverend Sister Dr. Annie J. Adams, PhD, affectionately known as my mama. Your faith, wisdom, and compassion are the seeds in my garden of life. My inspiration and faith are sprouts from you.

Contents

Acknowledgments

God deserves the honor and glory for giving me the vision for this book. I am blessed abundantly with the gift of writing and the ability to use humor and faith to encourage others.

Blessed am I to have a mother who put her projects aside to listen to me read, edit, and rewrite stories. You have taught me to chase my dreams and that anything is possible through Christ.

My two sons, Donovan and Joshua, it has been amazing to watch you grow into the young men you are today. You went from begging me not to include you in a blog post to telling friends, "My mother is writing a book." Thank you for providing a plethora of funny episodes for my writing.

To my friends in the pew—Heidi, Bertha, Ericka, Anna, and Tomika. You suffered through menopause right along with me. You didn't complain when I fanned you because I was hot. Nor did you frown when I bumped you while putting my jacket back on because I was cold. Thanks for accepting my *special* side of silly.

Many thanks to Adriene, owner and coach of A-Train's SuperFit, where inspiration and motivation lead to transformation.

Heartfelt gratitude to my college roommate Wendy, your insightful feedback gave birth to my stage name *Hott Flash*.

Flo, my *bestie* since high school, thanks for recording my skit on Menopause. This gave me the traction to push toward writing this book.

Thank you to my readers for selecting this book. You are the reason for my writing. May you discover a nugget of inspiration that will ignite a flame under your dreams.

Introduction

As I pushed pillows from my bed, threw blankets off my shoulders, and kicked my legs out of bedsheets, I screamed out, "Menopause ain't no joke."

I know that statement wasn't grammatically correct, but there were no language police present. It was at that moment I declared I would share my episodes of menopause in an effort to provide support to other women. Humor would be my tactic.

Humor is healing … at least that is what this author believes. Life gives us plenty of opportunities to become frustrated, annoyed, and discouraged. A dose of laughter injected right in the belly can diffuse those negative instances.

Annoyance is easily reached during the menopausal stage of life. It's like PMS (pre-menstrual syndrome) on steroids. What's a woman to do? Laugh in its face. If you have ever been hot one minute and cold the next, this book is for you. If you have ever had to narrow your eyes and talk through clenched teeth to your child, this book is for you.

The collection of essays contained herein were written with considerable prayer and reflection and sprinkled with humor. They are life stories of my unfolding journey of balancing menopause with parenting. You, or someone you know, may be experiencing this topsy-turvy season of life.

The title of this book was birthed from my participation in a pageant for women fifty years and older. Yep, you read that right—all the women were over fifty. There was no swimsuit competition, but we did have to perform a talent. I said, *Lord, what can I do as a talent?* After many sweaty nights and a few midday sweat sessions, I had my answer. Comedy. Menopause and comedy would be my routine for the pageant. And menopause *was* the joke for that evening.

The purpose of this book is to help the menopausal woman maintain a level of sanity while experiencing constant body changes.

This book will uplift your spirits and encourage you to put life's trials and tribulations into a healthy perspective by making them appear smaller. As you read the essays, repeat this mantra: "A chuckle a day keeps stress at bay."

Find something that makes you smile every day. You can have joy no matter your circumstances. Create a mantra that will encourage you. Know that you are beautifully and wonderfully made, sweat and all.

Love yourself through the hot and the cold seasons of menopause.

Menopause Rx

There is a prescription for everything nowadays. With every prescription there are side effects. This menopause Rx that I'm prescribing is no different. Read one chapter before bedtime; no eating or drinking while reading, as this could pose a choking hazard. That is your side effect—potential choking from laughter.

On an annual office visit, I mentioned to my doctor that I had started to sweat throughout the night. She informed me that if things became unbearable to the point that I was not sleeping, there was medication available. However, there were side effects. Her statement reminded me of a TV commercial about medications.

The TV commercial blared in the background as I was folding clothes. Medication for some aliment was being advertised. At the end of the commercial, all of the side effects were rattled off by an invisible announcer. "Could cause headaches, severe abdominal pain, may cause blood clots … *and* mild depression could occur."

My decision was to deal with the hot flashes. I don't need to pay to be depressed. I can just open my monthly utility bill.

It's enough to make you start singing, "Lawd, don't move my mountain, just give me the strength to climb."

Is there no balm in Gilead? Is there no physician there?
Why then is there no healing for the wound
of my people? (Jeremiah 8:22 NIV)

Humor Corner: Don't take it seriously!
Whatever you may be feeling today, it's best to write it down.

Reflections
Today, I am thankful for…

Hot Flash

Let me start by telling you what a hot flash is not. A hot flash is *not* a breaking news story. It is *not* a burst of light from a camera. If you've never experienced a hot flash, think of it like this: it's an intense feeling of warmth that can last a few seconds or several minutes.

Hot flashes have caused me to reconsider how I live my life. I know I don't want my eternal address to be 123 Hades Boulevard. When that warm sensation engulfs my body, it causes me to cry out, "Adam, don't eat the forbidden fruit! Run, Adam, run!" I feel like I'm being personally tormented because Eve led Adam astray.

If you experience this sudden change in body temperature, recognize it for what it is: a flash of extreme heat. Breathe through it. It will vanish soon.

> It will be a shelter and shade from the heat of the day, and refuge and hiding place from the storm and rain. (Isaiah 4:6 NIV)

Humor Corner: Don't take it seriously!
Whatever you may be feeling today, it's best to write it down.

Reflections
Today, I am thankful for…

Jesus and a Hot Flash Saved My Life

Snapping green beans at 8:30 p.m. should have set off alarms in my mind. Like a well-oiled machine, my body slows down and is asleep by 10:00 p.m. On this particular day, I made a smorgasbord of every food in sight—except vegetables.

The goal taped to my bathroom wall said, "Visualize a stronger, healthier you." I needed to get back on track. My plan was to add more vegetables to my meals for the next day. To accomplish this, I had to cook once I arrived home after working—and after spending two hours at my favorite writing spot.

Fresh, steamed veggies should be a *snap* to prepare, right? Not this time. After about twenty minutes, the green beans were not steamed to my liking. I let them cook a while longer. The beans cooked, and I slithered under the sheepskin spread on my bed, oblivious to the fact that the beans were still cooking.

In my weary state, I could have given Sleeping Beauty and Snow White a run for their money. I didn't bite a poison apple, but I was in a deep sleep for a couple of hours. In the blink of an eye, I was kicking covers off. My body temperature was rising with a hot flash brewing. I tossed and turned, and then a thought struck me.

I jumped from my bed quicker than the Gingerbread Man, burst from my bedroom, and bolted for the kitchen. There were no flames nor smoke—just a strong stench like scorched rubber. The green beans were still green. However, my boiler was black. As I washed the pot, flakes of sooty debris flew off.

If it had not been for the hot flash, I may have continued to sleep. I believe this was Jesus's way of saying, "Girl, you need to get up before you burn the house down." I'm so glad He watched over me.

Keep your lives free from the love of money and be content
with what you have, because God has said, never will I
leave you; never will I forsake you. (Hebrews 13:5 NIV)

Humor Corner: Don't take it seriously!
Whatever you may be feeling today, it's best to write it down.

Reflections
Today, I am thankful for…

Night Sweats

Night sweats are a series of hot flashes.

Have you ever gotten so hot you just start talking out of your head? It's like you're speaking in tongues. It may sound like this: "Shadrach, Meshach, and Abednego, Jack and Jill went up a hill to fetch a pail of water. Humpty Dumpty sat on a wall; Humpty Dumpty had a great fall. In Jesus's name, amen." You just combined the three Hebrew boys with your favorite nursery rhymes.

Night sweats are always annoying, no matter the season. It's never pleasurable to wake up soaking wet, as though you just participated in a triathlon. No need to experience anxiety; pray your way through.

> Do not be anxious about anything, but in every situation
> by prayer and petition, with thanksgiving, present
> your requests to God. And the peace of God, which
> transcends all understanding, will guard your hearts and
> your minds in Christ Jesus. (Philippians 4:6–7 NIV)

Humor Corner: Don't take it seriously!
Whatever you may be feeling today, it's best to write it down.

Reflections
Today, I am thankful for…

The Hokey Pokey

In the stillness of a dark room, while you are sleeping, menopause rears its ugly head. It materializes in the form of night sweats. As soon as you become comfortable, cozy, and snuggled under fleece blankets, a warm sensation takes over your body. The game begins; it's covers off, covers on, leg out, leg in. The hokey pokey, round one, has begun.

The hokey pokey is a game of movement of body parts. In the midst of night sweats, you are thrown into the game as an unwilling participant, flailing arms and legs in all directions. It's a phase women go through. We can play along and accept the game, or we can walk around with a pouty face and complain.

What will it be? Left leg in, left leg out, and you shake it all about? It's okay to play the game until this phase of menopause subsides.

> When I was a child, I talked as a child, I thought as a child,
> I reasoned like a child. When I became a man, I put the
> ways of childhood behind me. (1 Corinthians 13:11 NIV)

Humor Corner: Don't take it seriously!
Whatever you may be feeling today, it's best to write it down.

Reflections
Today, I am thankful for…

Hair

There is a pop song that contains, "I am not my hair" within the lyrics. I believe this truth to be self-evident. Hair threaded with strands of silver, bangs that are thinning, and the creative comb-over are all signs that your hair is beginning to change.

I used to wear bangs until one day I noticed that my hair looked thin. When I discussed this with a friend, she said, "Maybe it's your medication causing the thinning."

I said, "I'm not taking any medication. The only thing I'm taking is a multivitamin. And it's a gummy vitamin." I sought the opinion of another friend.

This second friend told me about a supplement she takes that's good for hair and nail growth. I tried the supplement and found it worked wonders. My nails were strong, and my hair—it was growing too. I just didn't know it was going to grow stronger above my lip and under my chin.

Why, even the hairs on your head are all numbered. Fear not;
you are of more value than many sparrows. (Luke 12:7 ESV)

Humor Corner: Don't take it seriously!

Whatever you may be feeling today, it's best to write it down.

Reflections
Today, I am thankful for…

Distracted Prayer

It always seems to be cold during church service, so I dress accordingly in long sleeves. As fate would have it, I usually end up sitting next to someone who is always hot. One particular Sunday I sat between two people who began fanning themselves, blowing cool air in my direction. It began during prayer. Our eyes were closed, and the breeze hit my neck and face from the left. I pulled my coat around one shoulder. Then the breeze came at me from the other side. I adjusted the coat and curled my shoulders inward.

After a few minutes, the breeze subsided, and I relaxed. I returned to listening to the prayer when I heard a sound coming from my left. I opened one eye, and the person next to me was opening her Christmas cards. Gently closing my eye, I resumed praying. It was short lived. The person on my right started coughing.

The coughing didn't bother me, but then the person from my left reached across me to pass a cough drop to the cougher. It was a symphony of distractions. I just gave up, opened my eyes, and began writing out this story.

> Fixing our eyes on Jesus, the pioneer and perfecter
> of faith. For the joy set before him he endured the
> cross, scoring its shame, and sat down at the right
> hand at the throne of God. (Hebrews 12:2 NIV)

Humor Corner: Don't take it seriously!
Whatever you may be feeling today, it's best to write it down.

Reflections
Today, I am thankful for…

The Dental Visit

The hard chair was in a reclined position. I rested my head against the back of the faux leather. My mouth was wide open. Dr. R touched my gums with his metal dental instrument. He asked questions as he gave special attention to each of my teeth.

"Has anything changed since your last visit?"

"Yes, menopause," I said.

"Oh, yes," Dr. R. replied, dragging the words from his mouth. "That can cause changes in your gums and teeth."

"Hmph, give it to me straight, doc. How much time do I have left with this set of teeth?" I asked.

He didn't give my teeth an expiration date. His cheekbones raised beneath the mask covering his mouth. A gentle smile was developing. I told Dr. R that from that point on I would be smiling every chance I got.

During a different visit, Dr. R examined my teeth further. He pulled and tugged on my cheek, touched my teeth with a gloved hand, and said, "Your teeth look great."

I attempted a gurgled response, and he removed his hand. I smiled and said, "Thanks." What I really wanted to says was, "My teeth should look good—I bought most of them from you. Crowns, caps, fillings, oh, my!"

And he said unto them, "Ye will surely say unto me this proverb, Physician heal thyself": whatsoever we have heard done in Capernaum, do also here in thy country. (Luke 4:23 KJV)

Humor Corner: Don't take it seriously!

Whatever you may be feeling today, it's best to write it down.

Reflections
Today, I am thankful for…

Menopause and Puberty

Is it possible to go through menopause and puberty at the same time? I'm not sure whether my body is part of some type of genetic experiment gone wrong, but there are a lot of different things happening at the same time.

I thought I was about thirty-five years past the acne stage. Not according to menopause. As I tossed and turned through the night, sleep seemed to poke fun at me. Finally, after a bumpy slumber, I woke up with a pimple on my nose. Yes, I went to bed with night sweats, and the next morning I awoke with a pimple.

What's worse, I learned that I was only in the premenopause stage. While I was in this state called premenopause, my teenage son was going through puberty. He was excited by this new stage in his life.

As I was riding in the car with my son when he was about fourteen years old, he looked in the visor mirror, rubbed his chin, and gazed at me. In his deep voice he said, "Ma, my mustache is growing."

I glanced at him and said, "So is mine, son. So is mine."

For God is not the author of confusion, but of peace, as
in all churches of the saints. (1 Corinthians 14:33 KJV)

Humor Corner: Don't take it seriously!
Whatever you may be feeling today, it's best to write it down.

Reflections

Today, I am thankful for…

The Hottest Season of Life ... Menopause

There's winter, spring, summer, and fall. Then there's menopause. It's the season where some women fan themselves when no one else is hot and say, "I'm experiencing my own personal summer." I used to hear women say this quite often. My reaction was a nonunderstanding smile. That is until I experienced a coming-of-age initiation of hot flashes.

You look out a frost-steamed window and see fluffy puffs of snow drifting gently to the ground. As you're inside, you're holding a handheld oscillating fan trying to find relief from the ninety-degree temperature of your body. Then quicker than you can say Rip Van Winkle, you shut the fan off because you're cold.

As seasons change, we learn to find the beauty in each bead of sweat, each drop of rain, and each cool breeze.

Let us not become weary in doing good, for at the proper time we will reap a harvest if we do not give up. (Galatians 6:9 NIV)

Humor Corner: Don't take it seriously!

Whatever you may be feeling today, it's best to write it down.

Reflections
Today, I am thankful for…

Nutrition—Food for Thought

It's expensive to eat healthy. I started a nutrition program with a group of ladies at the fitness gym where I have a membership. One of the ladies mentioned Ezekiel bread as something healthy to eat. I went to the store in search of this Ezekiel bread. At first I didn't even know what they were saying.

I found this bread in the organic section of the store, and the bread cost $5.99. Yes, $5.99 for bread that had the name of a prophet from the Bible. My thought was, *Is this bread expensive because it comes with a scripture or a prophetic word?* "Thou shalt not overeat." Was this the biblical version of a fortune cookie? I'm not comparing the word of God to a fortune cookie. Well, I am, but I'm not saying this as being superficial. Both include a message. The Ezekiel bread does, in fact, have a scripture reference on the package.

We need manna to keep our bodies functioning, just like a car needs fuel. Sometimes you may choose the midgrade gasoline for your vehicle; sometimes the high octane is your choice. Comparatively speaking, Ezekiel bread can be viewed as that high-octane fuel that you sometimes choose for your body.

> Take wheat and barley, beans and lentils, millet
> and spelt; put them in a storage jar and use them
> to make bread for yourself. (Ezekiel 4:9 NIV)

Humor Corner: Don't take it seriously!

Whatever you may be feeling today, it's best to write it down.

Reflections
Today, I am thankful for…

Etiquette for Eating Socially

Has most of your dining lately taken place at the drive-through or over the kitchen sink? If so, your social dining skills may be a little rusty. When you chauffeur kids from activity to activity, it's not often that you take time to hone your fine dining skills. And that's the excuse for my recent eating disaster.

Although I've attended many functions where food is served, while at a recent workshop, I lost a fight with a chocolate chip, cream cheese muffin. It happened during the continental breakfast. It was an informal setting, no tables, just rows of chairs set up lecture style.

As I broke off sections of the muffin, a chocolate chip went flying in one direction and a cluster of brown chunks in another. I changed my strategy and attacked the muffin with my plastic fork; moist bites of muffin finally reached my palate. A bite of muffin. A sip of Hazelnut coffee. A moan of delight slipped from my mouth.

The woman behind me took a bite of her muffin. "This is good. Is this what you have?" she asked.

I nodded in agreement and mumbled, "Mmm," trying not to talk with my mouth full. With a satisfied tummy, I dabbed at my mouth with a napkin.

It was almost time for the workshop to begin, so I dashed to the restroom to freshen up. Upon inspection of my face, I noticed a speck under my eye and another above my lip ... leftover muffin. I'm not quite sure how crumbs made it behind my glasses, but it was obvious I had not mastered the use of a napkin.

What is the etiquette for eating a muffin? I'm not sure, but I bet social eating blunders occur all the time.

Build houses and settle down; plant gardens and
eat what they produce. (Jeremiah 29:5 NIV)

Humor Corner: Don't take it seriously!
Whatever you may be feeling today, it's best to write it down.

Reflections

Today, I am thankful for…

Laughing through My Pain—a Teen and His Bedside Manner

There's Dr. Doolittle who talks to animals and Dr. Phil who gives advice, and then there's my teen son. He doesn't have the title of doctor before his name, but he tried to assist me when I was feeling ill. His intentions were good, but ...

One night I was experiencing stomach pains, and I had chills. I tossed and turned in bed, but could not get comfortable. Finally, I shuffled into my son's bedroom and curled up on his floor with my blanket. I hesitated to stay because he had the TV volume set to movie-theater, surround sound. I stayed because he had the space heater on.

As I moaned, my son asked if I wanted to take anything. I told him yes. He left the room in search of pain relief for me. When he returned, I heard drinking glasses clanging around, but minutes passed and he didn't bring anything in my direction.

"What did you find for me to take?" I asked.

"I couldn't find anything."

"But I heard you clanging glasses around like you were preparing something."

"Oh, I was just moving some things."

I rolled to a sitting position, dragged myself to my room, and found the last packet of Alka-Seltzer. I inched my way back to the warmth of my son's room. Handing my son the packet, I said, "Put this in water for me."

My son picked up one of the drinking glasses (which had already been used), filled it with water from the bathroom sink, and plopped the Alka-Seltzer in. Maybe he thought that in the dimly lit room, I wouldn't notice he'd given me a previously used glass.

This wasn't the first time we've used Alka-Seltzer for pain relief, so I assumed my son knew how to prepare it. The instructions say to dissolve the tablets in four ounces of water. Sometimes I use a little more to take away the aftertaste.

My son dissolved or perhaps diluted the tablets in a twelve-ounce glass of water and handed it to me. "Umm, Dr. Jekyll, this is too much water. First, a dirty glass, and now this. Are you trying to make me sicker?"

After my chills subsided, I broke out into sweat and returned to my room in search of sleep. My son didn't have the gift of Dr. Doolittle nor Dr. Phil, but he did have the ability to comfort. Next time a simple hug would be enough.

> Every way of a man is right in his own eyes: but the
> Lord pondereth the hearts. (Proverbs 21:2 KJV)

Humor Corner: Don't take it seriously!
Whatever you may be feeling today, it's best to write it down.

Reflections
Today, I am thankful for…

The Football Scrimmage

Commitment, dedication, devotion—these are the things my teen son focuses on during his high school football season. The same is required for parenting through football season. This was evident on the day of our first scrimmage of the season.

As I backed my car out of the garage, rain pelted the rear of the car. The sound of the drops increased in volume as the entire car emerged from the shelter of the garage. I adjusted my windshield wipers from slow to medium speed.

There was a scattering of parents sitting on the metal bleachers when I arrived at the football field. I walked up with my stadium chair strapped on my shoulder, an umbrella in one hand, and a blanket under my arm. This game was the blue-and-white game, where the varsity players scrimmaged each other rather than another team.

I stood along the chain-link fence with my rain gear, debating whether I wanted to stand or sit. I stood, rain bouncing from my umbrella and my eyes scanning the field for my son. There were no numbers on the players' shirts. I could not see my son's signature dreadlocks dangling from his helmet.

Heavy raindrops pelted my umbrella and dripped onto the back of my pants. Within minutes I was soaked and still searching for my son. I kept my eyes on the defensive players, wondering why I was there. I couldn't identify my son from the other players. Commitment, dedication, devotion.

Finally, I identified my son by his confident stride and blue Nike cleats. Mission accomplished. I saw my son maneuver a couple of plays, then shuffled my way back to my car. By this time, I felt like a toddler in a wet diaper. I just wanted to go home and change clothes.

Once in the car, I sat a few minutes to collect my thoughts. This situation deserved to be a blog post. The players began to leave the field. The game was called due to the rain.

My son walked over to the car and said, "I'm mad that they stopped the game. We barely played." For him, the rain was no obstacle. He just wanted to play. For this mama, I wanted a fuzzy bathrobe and socks.

I prayed for this child I prayed and the Lord has granted me what I asked of him. (1 Samuel 1:27 NIV)

Humor Corner: Don't take it seriously!
Whatever you may be feeling today, it's best to write it down.

Reflections

Today, I am thankful for…

Things Teens Don't Tell You

Sometimes being a parent is like becoming a detective. When it comes to teens, you have to dig, prod, and pull information out of them. It's easy for them to communicate when they want something, but when you want further information, they clam up.

Here are just four situations my teens did not tell me ... but I discovered. These are words that were never muttered, mumbled, or whispered.

1. I borrowed your car.

    When my son was home during a school break, he routinely went out for an evening run. Sometimes he would take his brother's car and stop by the store. As he left one evening, he yelled up the stairs to me, "Ma, I'm leaving. I'll be back in a little while."

    My son was out the door and returned within an hour, and that was the end of the story ... until morning.

    My son, who towers over me at six foot four, had borrowed my car. He left evidence. I told my son, "I know you borrowed my car."

    "How did you know? I didn't move the seat. I drove squished up," he said.

    "You changed my radio station," I told him.

    "Oh."

2. I may have lost a school book.

    It would have been nice to hear my son at least murmur those words above. However, it didn't happen that way. During fall registration, my son and I stood in line waiting to pick up his schedule.

Before we could proceed, a volunteer worker handed us a folded slip of paper that contained the sentence, "Balance due eighty dollars—lost book fee."

I told my son, "I didn't read that book, nor did I lose it. Why should I have to pay for it?" My voice elevated an octave. It was his senior year of high school. We had to pay the fee or risk him not graduating on time.

3. My lunch account is low.

Telling me that his lunch account at school was low would have been the easy thing for my son to do. Who wants to do things the easy way? Obviously not my son. Instead, he waited for me to receive a note from school stating, "Your child's lunch account is -$4.85."

4. I want a pet (that I'll leave for you to take care of).

During Christmas break my college son mentioned he wanted a dog. I suggested he wait awhile and think about the responsibility. I didn't hear any more talk of a dog. A week went by, and as I was relaxing with a book, my son phoned me and said, "Ma, we're picking up my dog."

The next thing I knew, a teen, his dad, and a dog arrived in my living room. The seven-week-old puppy was like having a newborn baby. She was pooping and peeing everywhere, and my son returned to school. He was lucky his little pal was adorable. She provided warmth as she slept with her paws on top of my feet as I typed at the computer.

I have learned to ask probing questions where my teens are concerned. Have you ever had to pull information from your child?

Listen my son to your father's instruction and do not forsake your mother's teaching. (Proverbs 1:8 NIV)

Humor Corner: Don't take it seriously!
Whatever you may be feeling today, it's best to write it down.

Reflections

Today, I am thankful for...

A Wrinkle in Time

My experience dubbed *A Wrinkle in Time* was the day my teen boys were running late for church due to wrinkled clothes. They dressed at the last minute and wanted to rush out the door. As my younger son handed me his shirt to be ironed, I looked down at his pants.

The black dress pants my son wore had creases at the knees from being on a hanger. He traded me his ironed shirt for the dress pants. No sooner had I finished ironing his pants than my older son walked past ... wearing wrinkled pants and shirt.

When I told my older son his pants needed to be ironed, he said, "These are wrinkle-free pants." Rather than fight another battle, I let him decide whether he wanted to iron the pants or not. He decided *not* to iron the pants. Instead, he substituted them with a different pair.

In the story *A Wrinkle in Time*, the characters traveled by *wrinkling* time. In other words they were able to travel quickly through space/time. It would have been helpful to *wrinkle* time the day we were running late. No such luck.

As I rushed the boys through the house barking demands, my older son said, "Ma, do you just wake up and plan what you're going to fuss about?"

After an outbreak of laughter from me, I responded. "No planning needed. You boys provide plenty of reason."

Although we were late reaching our destination, we ironed out our wrinkles. We learned a lesson. For me the lesson learned was to be sure to give the boys more lead time to get ready for an event. A lesson learned by the boys was, "Mama is going to grumble no matter what."

Perhaps you have experienced a time where you were running late for something due to poor planning.

> Be dressed in readiness and keep the lamps burning, like servants waiting for their master to return from a wedding banquet, so that when he comes and knocks they can immediately open the door for him. (Luke 12:35–36 NIV)

Humor Corner: Don't take it seriously!
Whatever you may be feeling today, it's best to write it down.

Reflections
Today, I am thankful for...

A Tale from Church Chronicles—A Tired Teen

It was a typical morning at my home on the first Sunday of the year. I made breakfast and then rushed around getting ready for church as my teen boys slept peacefully. After a short time, I yelled my warning into each boy's room, "I'm leaving in twenty minutes. You need to be ready if you're going with me."

One teen began to move, and the other pulled his covers tighter. I gave a final call announcing my departure. I left alone. Both boys are licensed drivers, and they rode together and arrived at church shortly after I got there. They usually sit as far away from the front of the church as they can.

On this particular Sunday, parishioners were packed in the pews shoulder to shoulder. The boys made their way up the aisle to where I was seated. They scooted past several sets of knees, then nearly sat on each other's lap in an attempt to squeeze close to me. The older teen conceded and settled in on the other side of me.

In a short time there were signs that the teens had stayed up late. My younger teen had his eyes closed and his head bowed, but it wasn't prayer time. When he lifted his head, he looked at me bleary eyed and said, "Ooh, I'm struggling to stay awake."

I whispered to him, "No, you've lost the struggle."

My son kept his eyes open a while longer, and then his head dropped again. This time I nudged his brother, who was seated on the other side of me. I said, "Should we wake him up?" His face broke into a grin and he shook his head no.

I decided to respond the way my boys respond to me—to ask for advice and then do the opposite. I gave my son's foot a little kick, and he lifted his head and said, "Did I fall asleep?"

"Yeah, you did," I told him. "Next time, when you lift your head, just say, 'Amen.' Maybe that way everyone won't know you were sleeping."

Later my son later reminisced about when he was younger and used to fall asleep on my shoulder or my lap. In my best singsong voice I told him, "You're a big boy now. You have to stay awake in church."

My son was tired because he had stayed up late. I was tired of struggling to keep him awake.

> Therefore stay awake for you do not know when the master
> of the house will come, in the evening, or at midnight, or
> when the rooster crows, or in the morning. (Mark 13:35 ESV)

Humor Corner: Don't take it seriously!
Whatever you may be feeling today, it's best to write it down.

Reflections
Today, I am thankful for…

Sneeze and Squeeze

Laugh, cough, or sneeze, you must keep your guard up. After a certain age, your bladder control may not be what it used to be. If you feel a sneeze coming on, you may need to squeeze your knees together at the same time. The impact of that sneeze, cough, or laugh could cause a trickle that no one else knows about except you.

It may seem like not long ago you were excited that your kids were out of diapers. Now you may need to go back to buying diapers, but not for the kids. Humph.

Remember your Creator in the days of your youth, before
the days of trouble come and the years approach when you
will say, I find no pleasure in them. (Ecclesiastes 12:1 NIV)

Humor Corner: Don't take it seriously!
Whatever you may be feeling today, it's best to write it down.

Reflections
Today, I am thankful for…

Being Recruited

Athletes are recruited all the time. My athletic abilities ended in the '80s (or when Jesus walked the earth, according to my kids). It was a time when my eyebrow hairs were brown and did not require an art degree to draw them on. My knees could still bend and glide across the floor in kneepads to dig for a ball smacked over the net in my direction.

It was long ago that I carried a gym bag stamped with my high school mascot and stuffed with my volleyball uniform. Now the only bags I carry are under my eyes. Yet, I was courted for a few years by AARP (American Association of Retired Persons). I was in my midforties when the initial invite landed in my mailbox. Gifts were offered. However, I wasn't quite ready to sign up. I felt like I could still be considered a youngster.

A few years passed, and another letter arrived. This time my signing bonus was the offer of a bag. It was smaller than the gym bag from my high school days but large enough to carry a few books, and it was stylish. They almost got me on the team. Then the thought occurred, *I have enough bags.* Between the bags under my eyes and the saddle bags on my rump, I didn't think I could carry anything else.

I was young, and now I am old. I have never seen the righteous forsaken or their children begging bread. (Psalm 37:25 NIV)

Humor Corner: Don't take it seriously!
Whatever you may be feeling today, it's best to write it down.

Reflections
Today, I am thankful for…

Menopause and Fitness

The experts say that engaging in fitness helps during menopause. For me it's at least an excuse for being hot and sweaty. The warm-up begins at home before I even make it to the gym.

I wake up sweating, cool down a few minutes, and then jump from the bed and get dressed to head to the gym for a more intensive sweat session. Before leaving for the gym, I take time for a little vanity. Did you know that as you get older you either lose hair or it becomes gray? Right now mine is in the graying stage.

To ride this wave of aging, one must become artistic. My masterpiece for this day was to draw my eyebrows on. This covered the gray and took a few years off my appearance. The only dilemma … would the pencil markings disappear as I began to sweat? It's a science experiment that I'll let you experience for yourself. Please share your results.

> Finally, be strong in the Lord and his mighty
> power. (Ephesians 6:10 NIV)

Humor Corner: Don't take it seriously!
Whatever you may be feeling today, it's best to write it down.

Reflections
Today, I am thankful for…

Faith and Fitness—Do You Have a Plan for a Healthy Lifestyle?

What do you do when you can't pray away the pounds? Change your prayer. If you've ever struggled with your weight, you know that there is no easy fix for reaching weight loss goals. It's hard work.

I've tried wishing the pounds away. "Lord, I sure wish I could lose seven pounds or even five." It didn't work. Then I prayed for the strength to get up each morning to make the drive to the fitness center.

Next, I prayed for courage to walk out of the locker room with my head up, even when the scale didn't display the results I wanted. In my mind, lights flickered, digital numbers rapidly increased, and then a warning flashed the message "wide load." This is when I realized that sometimes you have to laugh at yourself.

What does it take to jump start a healthy lifestyle? Identify your goals and make them measurable. Is your goal to eat healthier, exercise more, or lose weight by a certain date? You can do it by making small changes each day.

One goal could be, "I will snack on fruit today instead of chips." If your goal is to exercise *more*, what does that look like? If you like to walk on a treadmill, perhaps your goal would be to add ten minutes to the time you normally walk.

If you fall short of your goal, don't beat yourself up. Get through the day with a little positive self-talk and start over the next day. Come up with a daily mantra, "I am happy, healthy, and terrific," or scripture—"I can do all things through Christ who strengthens me." When you say this enough, you believe it and you feel better.

One thing I've learned as I continue to reassess, reevaluate, and rethink my weight loss/maintenance goals, it's not always about me. Sometimes your struggle can be a blessing to someone else.

The adult mime ministry at my church ministered to the song, "Not Me Lord, You!" by Paul S. Morton. When I compare this song to my weight loss issues, I just have to say, it's not about me. My lesson can be a blessin' to someone else.

If you are struggling with your weight, set a goal to change one thing tomorrow. I attended a seminar where the speaker asked us, "How do you eat an elephant?" The answer was, "One bite at a time." Don't be overwhelmed by the big picture. Break your task into smaller pieces.

No matter what … love the skin you're in. And while you're working out, you can pray for the strength to lift that barbell one more time. What will you do differently tomorrow?

> "For I know the plans I have for you, declares the Lord,
> plans to prosper you and not to harm you, plans to
> give you hope and a future." (Jeremiah 29:11 NIV)

Humor Corner: Don't take it seriously!
Whatever you may be feeling today, it's best to write it down.

Reflections

Today, I am thankful for…

The Ten Commandments of Menopause

1. Thou shall not steal thy neighbor's fan at church.
2. Thou shall not covet they neighbor's sweater when a hot flash arises and disappears.
3. Thou shall not adjust the temperature while riding as a passenger in another person's vehicle.
4. Thou shall not lie about experiencing the symptoms of menopause.
5. Thou shall not adjust the temperature when visiting a friend's home.
6. Thou shall comfort a fellow menopausal friend.
7. Thou shall recite the menopausal oath (this too shall pass) when feeling stressed.
8. Thou shall remain cool in hot situations.
9. Thou shall not kill thy neighbor's spirit while experiencing a mood swing.
10. Honor thy mother and sisters who may also feel menopausal, that your days may be more bearable.

Oh, how I love your law! I meditate on it all day long.
Your commandments are always with me and make me
wiser than my enemies. (Psalm 119:97–98 NIV)

Routine

Sitting in bed nestled under a blanket, I fell asleep with a book on my chest. After a short time, I popped one eye open and glanced at the clock—11:00 p.m. was displayed in red letters. It was past my bedtime.

A routine provides comfort and stability and eases stress. You may not even realize how easily you can slip into a routine. There are subtle signs that you have established a routine. Those signs may even alert you that it's time to change your routine.

Favorite coffee shop visit—I'm a coffee drinker and I have a favorite spot I frequent to write and enjoy my cup of java. My son was talking to a friend one day, and sometime during the conversation the friend said, "I know your mom ... small coffee, double cream, double sweetener." The cashier knew me by my favorite beverage.

Writing checks—I like to read. When a new book was released by one of my favorite authors, I dashed off to the bookstore to purchase a copy. At the checkout register, I pulled out my checkbook to pay. The cashier said, "Oh, you're writing a check? Not many people write checks any more, but your checks are pretty." Was my method of payment archaic?

I've learned that is okay to deviate your routine, break the norm ... or begin a new routine. What is one thing that you do routinely?

Jesus Christ is the same yesterday and today
and forever. (Hebrews 13:8 NIV)

Humor Corner: Don't take it seriously!
Whatever you may be feeling today, it's best to write it down.

Reflections
Today, I am thankful for…

Comedy in the Air

At the beginning of my airplane trip, a flight attendant came on the microphone and announced the routine instructions. He began by telling us, "This is a no-smoking, no-complaining, and no-whining flight." After an outburst of chuckles, he had our attention.

The flight attendant continued with his safety instructions. Some people were actively listening, while others were preoccupied with arranging their belongings. It was at that moment the flight attendant said, "Good luck to the six of you who paid attention."

I was feeling pretty much at ease with the comedic banter of the flight attendant … until it was snack time. Slightly famished, I was looking forward to a quick snack on the short flight. I had not flown in a while and wasn't sure the quantity and type of snacks I could toss in my carry-on. My favorite snacks were left behind.

After the *fasten seatbelt* sign flashed off, we were told that we could move about the cabin, and snacks would come around soon. It was also announced that since there was someone on board with a nut allergy, pretzels would be served. Totally understandable, until …

Just for fun. I dumped the pretzels onto a napkin and counted them. There were twelve micro, mini, miniscule pretzels. I craned my neck to see if I could find the funny flight attendant. Surely this was a part of his humor. Since it was a no-complaining flight, I munched my mini pretzels slowly, one at a time, to savor the flavor.

At the end of the flight, I thanked the flight attendants for their service and gave kudos to the pilots for getting us to our destination safely. Overall, I don't care about the snacks; I'm more impressed with quality service and a safe landing.

Everyone appeared to have followed the rules on our flight—no smoking, no complaining, and no whining. What comedic episodes have you experienced lately?

Sarah said, God has brought me laughter, and everyone who hears about this will laugh with me. (Genesis 21:6 NIV)

Humor Corner: Don't take it seriously!
Whatever you may be feeling today, it's best to write it down.

Reflections
Today, I am thankful for...

Family Funnies

What is the funniest thing a family member has shared with you recently? In my household there is rarely a dull moment.

At age forty-something I made the decision to get a retainer to correct one of my teeth. The first day I wore the retainer, I don't think my son noticed my speech was different. It was day two when he starred at my mouth as I was talking and noticed something was different.

"What is that in your mouth?" he asked, frowning.

"Do you mean my retainer?" I played dumb.

"Why do you have that at your age? Won't you be losing teeth soon?"

I guess I must not have read the age guidelines for wearing a retainer.

Our mouths were filled with laughter, our tongues
with songs of joy. (Psalm 126:2 NIV)

Humor Corner: Don't take it seriously!
Whatever you may be feeling today, it's best to write it down.

Reflections

Today, I am thankful for…

Open Letter to My Children— Make Room for Mama

This letter is dedicated to my teenage children for all the things they have done to make life … interesting. Bless you, my children.

Remember the times you said, "I can't wait to grow up"? Well, I'm not rushing you to grow up, but I look forward to many of your "first" experiences leading into adulthood.

I can't wait for you to get your first car. I'll be the first to ride in the passenger seat when you take it for a spin. We can stop by the corner store so that I can pick up a few snacks. When I'm done eating, I'll leave candy wrappers on the seat and let my beverage can roll under the seat.

After that we can stop by the pizza place and grab dinner and a lot of napkins that I'll leave all over your car. After stuffing ourselves, surely we will want to work out. I know how you like to stay in shape for sports.

We'll go to the fitness center, work up a sweat, and then shower there before heading home. You can stuff your damp, soiled gym clothes in my bag. I'm willing to share. No need to take the bag into the house. Leave it in your car. I'll get it after a few days. By then it should smell like a gym full of teenagers after gym class.

I'm not rushing your teen years because I love attending your sporting events and being a part of your high school years. However, I will be as excited as a tick on a dog with bushy fur when you get your first home. It would bring me joy to prepare your favorite meal. If you don't plan to be at home, just leave a key and I will let myself in.

Preparing dinner is sure to make me thirsty. I know how you like to keep a two-liter pop on hand. I'll just help myself to a glass, then leave the dirty glass at some random location in your house. If there is just a drop of pop left in the bottle, I won't finish it off. Instead, I'll return the almost-empty bottle to the fridge.

Once you arrive home, we'll have a casual dinner, eating from paper plates while sitting on the couch in front of the TV. After our meal, fit for a king, I'll be too stuffed to move. So, I'll just leave my paper plate on the floor near the couch or maybe even shove it under the couch for you to discover later. Each time I visit your home will be a reminder of the love we share and your desire to be grown up.

Love you, my young men. Be sure to make room in your life for Mama. Bless you, my children.

What would a letter to your child contain?

So in everything, do to others what you would have them do to you, for this sums up the law and the Prophets. (Matthew 7:12 NIV)

Humor Corner: Don't take it seriously!
Whatever you may be feeling today, it's best to write it down.

Reflections

Today, I am thankful for…

The Lighter Side of a Mammogram Visit

The reminder letter arrived in the mail. "Your mammogram is scheduled for ..." The letter included the things that needed to be done to prepare for the appointment:

- Arrive ten minutes early.
- Do not wear deodorant.
- Blah, blah, blah.

On the day of my appointment, I arrived as scheduled, checked in at the desk, and only waited a few minutes before my name was called. I followed the worker to the next waiting area. It was the area where the patient undresses from the waist up and places her belongings in a locker. And that is where my trouble began.

The clothing items fit into the locker with ease. However, when I tried to put my purse in the locker, it became wedged half in, half out of the locker. I gave the purse a shove, but it only moved an inch.

I had to devise a plan quickly. The staff at that doctor's office is efficient, and they don't leave you waiting long. When the technician returned for me, I didn't want to be standing there with my lovely gown swaying and me wrestling with the purse.

I removed a few items from my purse—small notebook, hand lotion, and fundraiser cards (my son's project). Then I reorganized other items—work cell, personal cell, Excedrin. Whew. Maybe I needed to clean out the entire purse.

The reorganization worked. I was rewarded with success. I tilted the purse and jabbed it a little, and it dropped onto the floor of the locker. I slammed the locker shut, removed the key and put the attached stretchy band around my wrist. I plopped onto a chair, breathless and sweaty, but just in time.

The technician entered the doorway. "Angela, are you ready?"

She took me to the exam room and did the exam, and I was back in the changing room within ten minutes. It took me longer to get my purse into the locker than it did to conduct the exam.

After my appointment, I thought of another point that can be added to the checklist of reminders for a mammogram appointment: Do not take a large purse.

When anxiety was great within me, your consolation
brought me joy. (Psalm 94:19 NIV)

Humor Corner: Don't take it seriously!

Whatever you may be feeling today, it's best to write it down.

Reflections
Today, I am thankful for…

Menopause Is ...

... wearing a sundress while everyone else is wearing winter clothing.
... finding the strength to smile through a hot flash.
... feeling like you're drowning in your own sweat.
... keeping cool in hot situations.
... being able to laugh at yourself.
... knowing that you are beautifully and wonderfully made.

Menopause is not ... the end of the world.

Nestled in bed surrounded by pillows, blankets over my shoulders, and legs curled tightly, I rested soundly. A hot flash disappeared, and I survived. So will you.

Humor Corner: Don't take it seriously!

Whatever you may be feeling today, it's best to write it down.

Reflections

Today, I am thankful for…

About the Author

Angela Verges is an award winning humorist (in training, waiting to be discovered). She has shared humor through blogging, women's retreats and other Christian venues. Angela is a graduate of Michigan State University and mother of two. She encourages the use of humor for healing and believes you can relieve tension, one laugh at a time. Find out more at www.angelaverges.com.

CPSIA information can be obtained
at www.ICGtesting.com
Printed in the USA
FSHW011300231120
76224FS